T0277844

Praise for John Hennessy . . .

"I can't say enough about this book, brilliantly and beautifully and generously shaped, ever alive in its language, a book of legacies and commitments, the poet's heart and soul and mind large with love, a book of a God who also exists within the poet's questions: 'Who reminds me I'm both father and son / and splits the sky unevenly between / the day and night? Who covers darkness / with a deeper dark? Who wakes me / with the light?' Rooted in immigrations and ancestral spirits, *Exit Garden State* takes us past refinery fires and Merck's slow clouds, Newark's steel flyway, Rahway prison's sullen grey dome, petrochemical winds across Route One and the human lives in these sites of destruction, a mill, a factory, a storage tank, a coker unit burned into the poet's essential self, back into and out of the poet's childhood into the childhood of his children, into his and America's present and future. Dantean in its depth, redemptively comedic, impassioned and compassionate, spirited and contemplative, *Exit Garden State* indisputably proves John Hennessy to be among the indispensable poets of his generation."

—Lawrence Joseph, author of *A Certain Clarity: Selected Poems*

"The title of John Hennessy's new book—*Exit Garden State*—is a brilliant clue to what lies ahead. We find haunting poems that call up the poet's childhood in New Jersey. We also see a more adult paradise lost: an exit from the garden of marriage and family, after divorce ensures a fall from the state of innocence. The tonal and formal range of these poems, now employing deliberate syntactic twists, now straightforward speech, and always a distinctive musicality, show us a poet with a remarkable gift to convey the ways that strong feeling can lead to wisdom."

—Mary Jo Salter, author of *Zoom Rooms: Poems*

"One cannot say, *Exit Garden State*, the title of John Hennessy's long-awaited third poetry collection, without first saying *exit garden*. Richly textured and enacting a finely-tuned music, Hennessy's collection explores his speaker's own similar departure from paradise (as well as the Garden State)—which necessitates transition, change, and loss, as his parents and sons grow older and a marriage dissolves. Vulnerable and formally dexterous, this fine collection manages to be haunted by personal history and all of that which we stand to inherit, and yet brimming, somehow, with hope."

—Nathan McClain, author of *Previously Owned*

EXIT GARDEN STATE

EXIT GARDEN STATE

John Hennessy

LOST HORSE PRESS
Scio, Oregon

Author Photograph: Ru Freeman.
Book Design: Christine Lysnewycz Holbert.

Copyright © 2024 by John Hennessy.
Printed in America.

FIRST EDITION

LIBRARY OF CONGRESS CATALOGING-IN-PUBLICATION DATA

Library of Congress Cataloging-in-Publication Data may be obtained from the Library of Congress.

ISBN 979-8-9890965-1-0

For my father,
Good in a crisis.

Table of Contents

If someone were to ask me what disaster this was that had befallen my life, I might ask if they wanted the story or the truth.

—Rachel Cusk, *Aftermath*

This is how you stand for a family photo,
look into the eyes of the photographer
the way you'd look into the eyes of a bird
perching outside your window:

remember me, wrathful bird's eye,
when we meet next time,
on the other side of this piercing—like a scream—life,
on the other side of anxious—like a stream—solitude.

—Serhiy Zhadan, "In forty years I won't talk in my dreams"

ONE · OIL TANK FARM

Family Man in the Valley

Hang the shovel from a Calvary
of nails. Resist your own cross-examination.

Ask the vine that creeps across the shed
to press its own advantage, vinegar of envy.

Approach child rearing as a farm-to-table
project. Think organic produce, grass-fed beef.

Or: clap like sunlight, wave hands like clouds.
Simultaneously welcome and release.

Scour the watering can caked with rust.
Pluck last fall's leaves still skewered on the rake.

Call the dangling branch widow-maker.
See who's first to wish it into firewood.

Middle School and Son

There's a ruined mill back there,
           where I'm headed this morning, upstream.
     In ten years I've gone
         from the forest's Iron Giant
  to Your Father the Car,
       swearing still—Jersey-style—
    at plodders, tailgaters.
               Ten years ago you'd
be hiking the woods with me,
            it's fiddlehead
     and trillium season,
         time for tiny white violets,

shoulder-stacked or piggybacked
        you'd have sprung
            yourself, coaxed me
                to the birch-bound graveyard
of old cars.   You'd banquet me,   cajole and caution,
   your turn to lead,
             boss,
               feed, a Triumph's rusted
         fender my supper,
     delicate as watercress or fern.
          And after, guzzle milkweed,
       chomp spikenard and beardgrass,
trample dogbane, bishopweed.

           Wild wormwood's taken me today.
   Even the dog's
         too old to come with me now.
And you're Burton

and Speke-ing
through the middle school.

Or Tarzan
of the mood swing, teeth
grit, texting me for rides,
love life lurching through
friend zone, gut ripped
twice before first lunch.

My beard of leaves grows,
grows over, and over.
Vines cover over my shoulders.
Finches flit along the wood's edge.
Purple martins.   Noiseless thrush.
Frogspawn in puddles.
Soon newts will red eft
out of the sinkhole, pass
skunk cabbage and punks,

the ruined mill
back here, where I'm headed
this morning, upstream,
to mull those stone walls
and sullen industry—
at your age, what didn't I know of sullenness?

My folks let me float
the Raritan, past refinery fires
and Merck's slow clouds,
Newark's steel flyway.

Oil Tank Farm

My love, your last gift is an oil tank farm, pitch-painted
dock, series of locks, slow chug up the Gowanus Canal
on an old iron fish, quick flight over Newark's brick walls

through Anheuser-Busch's blinking red A, fog-horn creep
and light's equivalent, the brewery's flapping white eagle,
red neon wings in electronic parabola, never-ending circle

over US Route One (Highways 1 & 9), a sutured, seamless
road along the oil tank farm's hydra-headed pumps, many-
eyed creatures, Argus unsleeping, or the watchdog's patron,

Cerberus on a leash: Eagle—A;
                                    Eagle, A;
                                            that sign flies again

over the nighttime sky of our own kids' childhood,
the Circle/A of dream's anarchy, they were safe on love's
loading docks, docks lined with container cranes,

bright capital-intensive ship-to-shore cranes with ample
storage space, but we've shifted away from the conventional,
the break-bulk terminal, you've given me unprecedented

maritime access, every day I marvel, unmoored navigate
darkened ports, this waterborne network of flatbed
boats, bulkhead slabs, the lifted and lowered train bridge,

my heart's pilot shack has a hole in the roof where sun
pours in, the seagull stands, osprey nests high-rising,
anticipating our unborn grandchildren, their kickball

fields and handball courts, stickball backstops with strike-zone
boxes they'll chalk themselves, in their playtime's backdrop—
a painted scrim—an empty tire plant waits, and, at night,

the brewery's neon eagle conspires with sodium lamps,
with brilliant silver towers and refinery fires, to illuminate
what you've left, make well-lit channels to this oil tank farm.

Family Story/So What Dad

In the family story, Dad's the first to college.
Five kids and nineteen years of three jobs later
he finishes a Ph.D. And shortly thereafter
goes solo. Our story starts in the New World
several times, most recently with the arrival
of his grandmother, Margaret Kinnane, from Lisdoonvarna,
County Clare. That town's heaven for singles,
cash cow for matchmakers. Every September
thousands of seekers cross the petrified Burren,
coming from all over Europe, all over the world,
to consult with marriage brokers. (New days
in the Old Country: recently The Outing,
a gay weekend, was added.) Beautiful in its rainwashed
way, the sun sudden on Norman ruins, Georgian stone,
but still my love teases: plaster Cupids aim
arrows over pub doorways, neon hearts blink
in shop windows. No surprise we ended up
on the Jersey Shore. Margaret came as a domestic,
fourteen years old; she took the family's single
boat ticket when her older sister lost her nerve
at the docks. We called her The Pit Bull—even I
knew her, she lied about her age, but lived late
into the 20th century—and we called her last
husband The Pussycat. My father refused
to go to her funeral, payback, decades after
she jilted her first husband, the Hennessy,
a bartender in Brooklyn, while he wasted in hospital,
dying slowly from an icepick in the eye.

So what if your father
doesn't call you back,
if you don't tell him
about your raise, or the play
your son wrote and directed,
or even the high school
stagehands who call him faggot
and threaten to beat him
in the stairwell—your precious child—
or the fury you stifled (your father's)
to let him as he insisted
handle his own affairs (and has he
even had any yet?),
how you didn't
call the principal, or better park your car
and wait after school for the punks
to walk by so you could warn them—
remember that childhood truncheon,
your souvenir Mets bat?
This is what you'll get
if it happens again,
in your quietest Jersey voice.
So what if you kept and still keep shtum,
good for you, and your Jersey voice,
which after all isn't a Brooklyn Irish
waterfront naze like his
but your own hangover
from those days of keeping it quiet
and mean and scared

But that's only our most recent arrival story.
My father's other grandmother was a Kettle,
and her folks immigrated earlier. Recently
her family came to us to fill in branches
in their tree, and there were a few surprises.
Grandmother Kettle's family-owned farmland
in Artane, were thick with Parnell even after
O'Shea's betrayal, agitated in the Land War
and suffered imprisonment at Naas
and again at Kilmainham, ran guns
from Belgium to the Irish Volunteers in '14.
In the middle of it all is Tom Kettle,
the only person James Joyce would talk Aquinas
with, from Clongowes Wood right through
to UCD. An MP, professor, and poet. Statue
in Stephen's Green: he died in 1916. Not
in the Easter Rising, but at the Somme.
He fought the Germans in an Irish regiment
of the British Army and worried he'd be
remembered as a traitor. In our family story
he never went to school or to war, never wrote
a book, held a gun. We would have saved him
from being remembered at all.

in the liquor store parking lot
behind your old building after he'd
shoved you back outside to fight your own
damned fights, that milling of older kids
from Shotwell Park you insisted
on pitching to, so what if you lifted
a chunk of the rotting tarmac
and hit a kid older by a couple years
in the neck with it, far as you could reach,
so what if you came home
bleeding through your crewcut
and your father took you to Stewart's
for a root-beer float
to celebrate? So what if he
doesn't call you back, so what?
Just as the sun
rises on your son he's proud
of you, he's all orange neon
diamonds and soda
and sticky picnic tables,
and the hornets
buzzing for you.
Or text him. Uncork champagne emoji.

No Clock in the Forest

—As You Like It

Come put a face to the name, Terror,
and if there's any grace left, it's terra.

Know you through the orange berries
of creeping bittersweet. Or twining worries,

woods end in wild grape, poison ivy, and woodbine,
birch saplings taut as bows, recurved by vine.

Grace, Terror, time to split the difference,
change tense, shift the seed, revel in fence.

Best-case scenario, I'm first to pass,
urn spilling over peonies, foxgloves, crabgrass.

Bring morning glory mourning's story,
Jack's pulpit cups, stamen's golden fury,

your aphids, vespids, narrative retreads.
Come, Terror, with overwatered flowerbeds

scattering dropped petals. Those fat grubs, loaded
spores. Panicked rose, potted beetles, eroded

root tags and graceless bees. Your face the same
old clock, obscured by sun, concealed by rain.

Convenience Store Aquinas

7-Eleven's a misnomer, like "mind-
body problem." They never close. The hyphen's

a dash of form. Sure, *this* mind-body's
a machine, if you want, plowing across town

to the steakhouse. American Spirit. Give us
the yellow pack. No matches? This dollar

fifty-nine Santa lighter too. Big-Grab bag
of Doritos. No, the "engine" is not

separate—it's part of the machine. Sure, paper's
good, container for recycling. Rain's no problem.

I eat the Doritos, smoke up—one for you?
The chips are part of my machine—

matter inside matter—smoke fires my lungs,
gives me that slap of pleasure in my

tailbone, maybe stimulates a thought.
I'm prime matter informed by the soul.

No, I didn't just slip the word in there:
that's a spade—it digs through bullshit.

Lean close, under the awning, cover up,
you want a light. The mist can't decide

if it's rain or fog. Streetlight moons, clouds
around the neon signs. Pink as the steak

we're heading for. The comfort of a red leather
banquette. No, your engine exists as part of

and powers its machine; separated, both are just
scrap, bunch of gears, rusty sprockets.

An unlit oven. Unbaked potatoes. Sour cream
inside a cow, chives growing mostly underground.

"Engine" is a bad analogy. I'm one thing,
not two. No intermediaries. I don't

have a body, I am one. A hungry
one at the moment. What'll it be?

Filet mignon? Slab of prime rib, don't trim
the fat? Twelve oz. T-bone, two inches thick?

No, I'll wait until after I eat for another,
but you go right ahead. Here's a light.

Back Home

Jack-pine cones, maple leaves, red tail-feathers
from a startled hawk—she filled her purse

with figments from the bulldozed woods.
Ice in the birdbath, a frozen millet stick.

Paint peeling from deck rails was too thick
to ignore. The colors matched her moods,

grey-blue on top, white oak below. The nurse
for evening meds, and maid at angelus. Red leathers

scuffed, spit-shined, roughed up again, the heels
a stack of wooden nickels. Mother's meals

grew smaller every day, rice grain, breadcrumb,
soon she'd fit on the head of a pin, too frail

to hold a lapdog, Siamese cat, the dumb
and artless jib that kept her rigging, sail

set to a constant circling—sickroom, kitchen, bath.
Propped up on pillows, mother watched the last

blackbirds harass the feeder. She folded sums
across her thoughts. Reckonings. Junk mail.

The clacking in the hall, her favorite boots,
hair still heavy on her shoulders, dark, loose.

13

Open Season, 2016

This afternoon there's shooting in the woods.
I can hear blasts from my kitchen. Veterans
Day. Too late for game. Asserting, celebrating
upset victory. They're too close. It's unnerving.

The boys are safe, at least—one's at college,
the other rehearsing. To the side door, see what
I can see. Some rodent has chewed the pumpkin,
weird prayer/offering to my grandfather—DAV—

on our deck. There won't be an ours much longer.
Fidelity is an alternative fact, but, for now, I'm left
with Grandpa who got dispensation from his dying
father to fight Sicily—he saw war coming in the Thirties.

Grandpa only made it as far as New Guinea: grenade,
back injury. In and out, the rest of the century,
VA hospitals. Tough old SOB. Took him years
to be "made"—Supervisor at the PO—

because he wouldn't join the party. Ilya,
from Serbia, formerly my uncle, explained
when I asked why Grandpa Cusumano—
three jobs, Elizabeth triple-deckers, tiny prefab

house around the corner from Merck, ten kids,
on official forms checked not "white" but Other—
was a Republican: "Grandpa's no Republican,
John," Uncle Ilya said. "He's a fascist."

Obedience, loyalty, respect, family: solution
to everything. Beat his sons, beat his daughters.

That last black eye took him to Carrier Clinic. Me,
the worst I got was my mouth washed out with soap—

what'd I say, was it *I want?* He was devoted to me.
I loved and I love him and I miss him. I Hail
Mary this afternoon, head into the woods hoping
the dogs run, that the gun-shots quiet down.

Leaving the Garden

Don't underestimate the power of the house.
Keep it, and keep the power. Or maybe you've
always had the power, so keep the house.
Surround the garden with painted fire, a grove
of burning maple trees that bend and close
behind the one who leaves. Let them leave
willingly, thinking another paradise grows
outside archangel flames, catalpa trees
will spread above the silver birches, rise
and flower, drop their pods on greener grass
or richer soil, all real, no artifice,
the constructs, contracts, whatever used to pass
for life, exposed. You'll keep the children past
childhood, the children's children, yours at last.

TWO · DOMESTIC RETROGRADE

Tutor to the Prophet

At play, James kicks pigeon-toed, legs
scissoring flared pants quick at the hips
and waist, white high-top Cons launching
a loud pink kickball arc—*p'ang*—
over Nova and Impala, parked Firebird,
ancient Valiant jacked up on the corner.
From third I can walk home backwards.
Rafael scores. James sprints behind, fist
of his pick raised from back pocket.

James at work we dub Wheejee, mad smart
at math and plants. Whole summer days pass
and we can't find him—he's hidden in the library,
spelunking the stacks, or tutoring his brothers.
The signal he's back? We see the aftermath
of his projects: he's window-boxed marigolds
and basil, peppers and geraniums, two kinds
of ivy, scented dianthus, shaded impatiens, or strung
clotheslines across the backstairs in zigzags,
maxing the surface area for laundry in the sun.

Later, on that same backstairs sunporch,
sheets sailing their lines around us, James—
our Wheejee—becomes Abdu Raheem.
The Autobiography of Malcolm X presides,
door-guard *Two Speeches*, bedside *the recitation*.
He debates Rafael on power, on the beautiful,
hegemony and difference. The apartment window
soundtracks low "I'd Rather Be With You,"
and his mother pinning her uniform before work
still overhears. Couple of Catholic boys, family
from suspect islands—Ireland, Puerto Rico, Sicily—

shit, jokes not James, nor Wheejee, but Abdu
Raheem, *should I just cut you two loose?*

Don't even kid, his mother says, opening
the back door on us, in the syndicated fiction
of memory, recast as Julia, say, Diahann Carroll,
or Rosalind Cash, volume rising, extra-
terrestrial, the hardwired guitar, Bootsy's
synth-like bass, braids gathered overhead
in one hand, blocking the skyline of Merck
stacks, Rahway prison's sullen grey dome.
You're going to do this thing, okay,
commit to the book. But where you three
go, let's ease back a bit, be circumspect.

(thirty years later, music down, clean laundry
billowing, snapping, construction site on the corner
quiet, sometimes I slip backstairs, in conversation
with her, with Ralph, lost Wheejee, wondering
aloud, imagining all over again his laugh
or scowl—as Abdu Raheem says)

Check
the tutor to the prophet—his work runs green.
Like mine. Al-Khidr. His name means green forever.
His mother turns back, fixes her collar.
We fold up sheets, bring them in behind her.

Netflix Green Man

Netflix The Green Man and any screen
becomes a vineyard. Episodes cluster
and climb, trellis narrative. Between
the corn and tree line creepers muster

nine lives. They grow, divide, and splice,
steal scenes by running fox grape, bittersweet,
return on any handheld device
as moonseed, woodbine, dodder, buckwheat—

false buckwheat—note, though star- and heart-shaped.
He trucks some mascot for our kids, glad-hands
a sidekick dressed to burrow, root, and take
them through their lessons rattling dad's

bouzouki nerves, mom's percussive bones.
Return, that ritual button, pressed like wine
in HD, when end credits jolt. Stop time,
we're keyed up. Eternal return? Eternal jones.

Leading with My Wedding Ring

It's all you: the reason I'm running in the first place,
not the jacket hanging in my closet, bespoke, too tight
for me, train whistle, rain through woods, the pace
I quicken when you become a branch breaking right
above, advice I take—to never mind, just trace
a new path beside the hemlocks, but beware the bite
of oaks, black cashmere with onyx buttons, brown cones,
green needles in the pockets. You're the trace of silk,
the truce, I mean, the silken truce, unsettled bones
near the coyote's den, the meal made mother's milk—
the castoff pelt becomes my running suit, the stones
I carry keeping me grounded, castle to your Rilke,
yours still, despite the totems loosed at me,
Stag, Cougar, Bear, Boor, some outrun easily.

Crane Elegy

How should we think of you now? Have you
taken your place near Gobekli Tepe, the temple
older than agriculture? Which of its carvings
captures you best? The white crane flapping

over the meadowlands, or the fish clamped
in its beak seconds ago? There's a scorpion
cut into the temple column, agamas climbing
over the stone. The ruins may as well hide

a Coney Island funhouse, while the crane
you've become circles the river mouth.
Forget the afterlife's scabbards and totems,
here you fly low over husks of cars, flatbed trucks

and salt-grass bales, your wings angle out
toward Staten Island, pitch under bridges,
over tugboats and barges. Back to boardwalk
crowds and taxi ranks, the traffic stopped

and convertible car-tops down, *Bird's Best
Bop* on satellite radio. You're in this signal,
the bass and snare, 360 degrees around
the saxophone rim. You shimmer and circle

and fly on, over nightclubs at Brighton,
Tatiana's, Primorski's, The Velvet Rope's
samovars and herring, knish stands and Nathan's,
deep fryers spattering, out to the tide line

and up to Jones Beach before sunset. You scout
the last crowds there, spiral umbrellas, skimboards

and body surfers, before sheering west to the Sound,
where we lose you in the sun. We'll speak of you

as you were: end of day, guard stands tipped over,
the band shell quiet, changing booths empty,
and you're a young man still riding surf
long after the last bathers have gone.

Miguel Hernandez Green

—with a line by Rafael Alberti

Even riding streetcars through Madrid
your wet roots showed, made running boards
damp, the ticket-taker slip. Everywhere

you brought with you a hillside restless
with goats, the nightingale from the Levant.
Birds sang joking through you all day.

You climbed trees in city parks, shook loose
golden leaves and green caterpillars, walked
the undersides of clouds in rope-soled shoes.

The thunder came from long-range guns,
and for you lightning never ended. Blood
shone common as light. You buried your dead.

Who would be left, it seemed, to bury you?
I'm old enough to be your father now.
And I'd care for your wife, my daughter,

make son my grandson. Let me replace
the father who abandoned you to prison.
When you died there, your eyes wouldn't close.

I'll visit with you in the woods each morning,
where your head still throws off a sound
of green leaves covered with flashes of light.

Silvano

But here's Silvano, half stooped, half
squatting, under a stand of hemlock, quiet
as a projection, his wolf hybrid

loping and darting, worrying long
circles, widening the route through
the woods where I'm running, Silvano's

match in quiet, ears pricked, yellow fur
sprung, tail in the balance, sprinting, flushing
doves, fallen birch leaves. My anxiety flares

before vanishing. Silvano's hunched
over a stump as if feeding. He straightens
and sees me, dirt and pine needles caught

in his hair, the long moustaches
he smooths when he engages. Underneath,
he looks like me, carries ancestry from Cyprus

and Sicily—dark, but eyes light
as the wolf hybrid's—and once we're talking
I don't pinpoint, fix the language. He's found

an old rubbish heap, smooth-necked
glass bottles, prescription vials, wire hanger,
plastic soldier. The trash has its mystery, signal

sickness and thirst, afternoons improvised
with little novelty. Staten Island boy,
Silvano, he worked at the refinery

ten minutes down Route One from me.
Silvano and I are both surprised
to be crossing these woods, passing

and living here, complain of the cold
and cool people—Nouveau England,
he says, his tone full of variety.

Yes, and in passing, I've never asked
what brought or keeps him here, and today's
no different. He pockets the soldier—whose

child in mind?—nods after a hunting
party half a mile uphill, shows me
a grouse feather that's mottled and bloody.

Silvano doesn't worry. He whistles
and the dog comes crashing but keeps
distant, all wolf and no petting. Days

to turn back, stick to the brook below,
shotgun blasts up the mountain, whine
of ATVs, wheel ruts in mud, my flash

of orange sleeves, the shouts and strange
silence. And there are days I'm afraid
of Silvano, his quiet and odd green camo,

convex mirror and wolf hybrid.

Panic Through the Refineries

Jersey driving   my sons Xmas-visit their mother
north up north   up the Connecticut River
only me flashing in and out   the white shock

the oil tanks and steel staircases enormously
circling   vault and scaffolding   another belch
of steam   stack after stack   a white cloud

I'm here   not here   I'm here   the air
so frigid this New Year   petrochemical steam
condenses   vapor to fog   white lights stud

my vision   Turnpike ice   the white sky draining
side of the road snow   the train over flatland   dark
creek   clean line   quiet curve click clack   but I

drive   this white car disappears   even the slow
lane speeds   I can see   I can't see   I can see   I'm
coming from my mother's   driving out of myself

my own childhood   and back into it   out of mine
and into theirs   I'm here   catalytic towers   out
of mine and into theirs   coker unit   not here

they're north up north   tires whump the highway
seams   in front and behind and on both sides
the lights and   steam   and snow   the long bridges

Dad Cried a Lot

Dad cried a lot as a baby, his mother told him. One time they decided to let him cry it out all night. In the morning, when she went to him finally, his bottle had rolled to the foot of the crib. They were glass bottles in those days, and this one broke and cut his feet. It could have been much worse.

Years later she told him she couldn't remember what the advice was then, because it was periodically changing in the post-war period—let the baby cry, put the baby stomach-down to sleep, don't feed the baby outside of the schedule—but she realized that he was probably hungry, that my father cried so much, so often, because he was hungry.

I remember coming into that house as a child. We went often and it was always the same, a small sad house on the outskirts of Rahway, where my father's father wasted and died. Hot in summer and cold in winter. If we went in the evening, after supper, it always smelled like burned food, burned meat, the cheapest cuts of beef, burned.

Of course I'm leaving things out, how much and how quietly my father loved his mother, how in mid-life I finally realized that he must have been her favorite, how she used to save money for him to play poker in the local game because he won, he always won, infuriating his father that she gave the money to her son and never to him.

Sometimes if I go out after cooking with my cast-iron pan, when I come home to my apartment it still smells like my food—ribeye fried in onions, or a thick sirloin seared and tender—but underneath I smell the ghost of that unhappy house.

More Sky Please

More sky please push open the apartment shutters
crowbar the paint factory's broken window frames rip
tarpaper from the caving roof push it back crack it open

blast an airshaft through the neighboring buildings snap
it back expose the bird-ridden drafts the wren's been busy
here mornings year round churr and chip golden open-throat

yodel smack in the sleep cycle soldered to feeder suet
in ivy like titmouse chickadee refusing to shift it back
Carolina Canada climate haywire more sky please *rik tik tik*

break open more light all the way past oil tank farms
creosote docks the Kill Van Kull slide by kingfisher flap
past cormorant incongruous flights parallel and merging

plunge into slap out of tidal pools the Fresh Kills beak
full of killifish and silversides crayfish and krill tarp
past the saltgrass and bridges fly Pulaski Skyway

Bayonne's silver buildings blank tower-blocks sky
wide as the river-mouth more sky more please push it back
past tankers and tugboats the last hulking cruise ship

lasers fired across a spinning disco ball wobble bass
and echo chamber dancing on deck past clanging buoys
waveless channels to deepest basin all things even

terns drop away sea and sky open wide and empty

In Another Life

In another life, I join the hierophants
of New Jersey, drink petrochemical winds
swirling across Route One, a new Delphi,
speak their ethylene mysteries. Called back

by my inexorable childhood, it becomes
impossible to ignore my sons' own strange
gifts: smokestacks stop smoking, chimney
fires burn green as pine, then flare out.

Miracles like this don't happen back home
in Massachusetts, so we pigeon feather
for a message, begin initiation. Windmill
camphor pots, magnesium mist our wrists

and foreheads, burn sage then sandalwood
then palo santo in blue ceramic bowls
bubble-wrapped back from Sifnos.
The singular past and several futures

never go dark here. Even summer
thunderstorms illuminate oil tank farms
destructive as divorce, and the vats
speak with a rumbling of their swollen

bellies, murky riddle. Don't go barefoot—
there's a snake in the grass, and Orpheus
sails in too late for the wedding. Wetlands
make for wet hay. The boys receive

instruction to draw forth superheroes reckless
as gods, cunning in combat with climate change.

Vines snake across the refinery, the earth
quakes and turns up old growth trees

and ferns, a flask of jenever. Pour a gulp
in the Arthur Kill for the guerilla war-dead
of family battles, we calm our restless
ancestral spirits, liberate them one by one

from petroleum tombs. They fly off
through ethylene vapor, escorted by heroes
the boys create, better heeled than Jason, think
a gracious Achilles, smoother than Perseus—

tongue cuts cleaner than the sword. I embrace
both boys as they grow to men, launch their barks,
thank them through words stark as smokestacks
for light they bring to senseless dark.

THREE · SECOND-CHANCE DAD

Second-Chance Dad

The second time my father gave me life
he pulled me from a coach's path. New York-
crossing, I stepped off the curb looking left, not right,
near Dublin's Rotunda. Exactly the mercy work
my sisters sent him for: grief's traffic fumes,
a useless creeping half-knowledge, had dulled my sense.
Dad, good in crisis, kept me fed, made room
for pints, told stories, boosted me over the fence
around Sheela-na-Gig, subject of my research.
Imagine otherwise: the site off limits,
retreat to books, hikes near the flat in Christchurch
(where they'd already trysted), steeped in ignorance.
What if I had avoided relatives, dead
in Dublin, living in Clare, just poxed and read?

Pay Packet Saturday

An Aisling for Sunim

Remember Saturday pay packets? Adrenaline
wildcat, dopamine stevedore, six shifts
in cash. Weekly tidy slick brown envelope, neat
stack of bills: five tenners, four fivers, or six

and two, two and ten. Heft of seven-sided coins, crisp
single notes. Red, brown, or grey-green background,
Medb or Swift's joyless portrait, some other liver-
tapped patriot, Lavery's Kathleen uniform watermark.

We'd scoot prams and strollers bellied over
from the Rotunda—how pregnant women
drove our ex-boxer boss Mick Blake crazy!
His solemn Saturday handshake, the one day

per week we loved him, 70 quid's worth
of gush, 63 hours in the Kingfisher basement
banging out baskets of chips, chunks to mash,
top of the pots. 70 punt was 52 pints.

Or 80 bags of crisps. 60 jugs of milk. 40 sticks
of fish. Block of blond hash to split six ways—
the Auld Dubliner's skinhead in the jacks.
My quarter of rent for the month, our flat

up over the hairdresser's on Dorset, a real thug
panorama: kids whistling Dixie and fat Yankee
Doodle behind us, then the policed quiet past
Sinn Fein HQ. Safe with our pay packets, safe

all the way down O'Connell, the river,
the quais, the rank Goths of Grafton Street
already drunk in the Pyg, all our young friends,
Hugh the architect, clean Christian Brother Saul,

Marie in red curly Mohawk cursing the scrubbers,
Leda who aced *The Leaving*, would love to study
literature, spec the Russians, only her folks'd
kill her if she left the Civil Service, processing trends

in parking tickets. Gin-drinking bored young
Leda who took me to bed and didn't mind
discomfort, called herself a punk Akhmatova—or
Nastasya Filippovna. Tender—no Idiot—I knelt,

went down lovingly in hideous sheets, a dusty
private hostel room on Frenchman's Lane. Saturday
next her friend Nessa said—hand on my crotch—
Ah you want to, see, her low smoking laugh, while

Leda stopped in the bog. Nothing to do with me
I knew so tied my own tail, got out of the way
on a pay packet Saturday. Flexed my pocket,
still half my pack left. Palm full of shrapnel, smash,

the cupric smell of it. Sunim! I sought your counsel,
a sprint through cold. So what if I silenced myself
later, we were flush with cash, flush and righteous,
next round's on me—and malted vinegar crisps.

Lenten

White Christmas lights blink in the sun,
the redbud tree still hung with ornaments.
Two crows, three grackles, haggle. By design
or chance, a totem cross wards off the torments

of winter's purchase, a pair of wind-jammed sticks.
Now grackle guns go off two fields away
launching a cloud of seed-fed birds. Old tricks,
same end. *Same, same,* the crows ungoverned spray

anxious, drill-bit spondees, wheel and drive
the grackles from our tree, then huddle dumb
and ominous, foil to the bed of white
Narcissus blooming below. Vanity's one

appropriate turn this time of year, its tropes
as vulgar as these birds. Time to take down
last season's trimmings, tighten the feeder's ropes,
while grackles return, filling the yard with sound.

Contagion! / Divorcing Dad

Contagion! The divorcing dad, new to the cul-
de-sac, with his teenagers on custodial split.
See how he weeps and eats before they wake up—
ah they sleep late—he pushes around
his oatmeal, winter berries, sugary maple,

toothache even to think—don't think, just eat,
eat. Bad luck: it could be catching: better hide,
hide your family. Oh, the towering spruce, leafless
oaks, snow on short streetlights, quaint carriage-
lamp tops, Frank Lloyd Wright ranches. His fog

of grief, cloud of smoke, morning coffee
and cigarette, you can smell him across the street.
He's fallen off his wagon, he's stunned, poor guy,
he doesn't know what hit him. The landscaped
pond, Adirondack chairs in snowdrifts, morning

wren throat rocking, Double-D strides around
laughing, crying, marveling at his temporary digs,
the wood floors, smooth closing drawers, mock
granite counter, the kitchen island. How he loves
an island. How he feels safe and can breathe

on an island. Ah the wide windows opening
onto bird feeders full of juncos and cardinals,
the red and the black, the deer tracks. Birdsong
brings Freddy back, the teenager who groped
him, undressed him, is he really dead, have

the birds brought messages from him, back
from the dead, king wren? Brown oak leaves skate
across the snow. How his wife insisted Double-D
tell their children:
                    It was cold outside, playground
wind-stripped of kids, beer cans crushed

along the cyclone fence, the apartment buildings
full of yellow lights, when Freddy took us down.
Your mother blames his touch for my
anxiety. I always needed to know where
you were. I called it good parenting. Truth

is the holes in memory. What came next?
What's next, king wren?
                    Tea-kettle, tea-kettle—
All the kids on the block, even my four-
year-old neighbor, what a collector.
Should I just say, *Boys, I've been undone?*

Tea-kettle—you may be mad with grief
but how quickly you compose yourself
when there's movement inside, your sons
rising, drawer opening in the next room,
faucet running, wren hopping, calling.

Cerberus vs. *Freddy*

Freddy towed me out to the refinery
shadow, drain spout gargoyle crouched
over his handlebars. We watched the sun

set through blue fire, gyro-spin
around baskets stitched from silver pipe
and ladder. The old guard dog spread

broad Rottweiler shoulders, stretched
its chain barking, foam in its muzzle.
Freddy dared me to pass my hand

through the fence. Even before teeth,
before snout snapped down, he had wrist-
rocket cocked and drawn. Startled

yelp; stunned howling. Blood came thick
as mucus, nearly clear, dog's-eye blind
and blinking. All that chrome machinery

flushed pink for a moment, red reflected sun
sunk through silver hoops. Beautiful,
Freddy said, but something always spoils it.

Whiskey Green Man

—Rosslyn Chapel to Glasgow, Friday night

That head's a wicked planter. Stone vines shoot
from every orifice, wreathe his neck and hands,
mouth stuffed with hawthorn leaves. Green, moot,
gushing silence. But he'll bark it down in iambs,

anything to help me understand: concuss,
concuss. Trip me on stairs, ass over shoulder,
fix seven staples, a lidocaine fuss
across my scalp. I'm already older

than trepan's laureate, Apollinaire—
still drink up life *comme une eau-de-vie*,
freak-chute the Zone? Sure, I'll read his stare
a hundred ways—he comes close to me—

play Baptist, slapstick, maythorn, steno, stitch
my bloody collar to thanksgiving screed,
a lesson to this Glaswegian itch,
a reassessment of want v. need.

Pink slash. Seven staples. A livid strand
of puckered skin from dome to neck. Soft touch,
dumb luck. Mouth shut? Not me. This land
our Móraí crossed in Hunger spooks too much.

Hospital zoot. *Nae bother.* My bunkmate blocked
shots from a broken bottle, handcuffed tight
both sides—laughing—to laughing cops. Take stock.
Heads up. Pillow's blood-soaked, but I'll be right.

Living the Dream

I reminded myself early in the day,
Don't forget your passport. So of course
I'm at the airport without my passport.

Less than two hours until the flight left
and it was international, so I was already
an hour late. Luckily, my son

was dropping me off. He could help me
with my phone, which was frozen, stuck on
an app, an image of a red album cover. Spotify.

I was deep into trying to call my father,
good in a crisis, someone I could rely on
to bring my passport. They'd get me out of this

red album cover anxiety, this disaster. The plane
would leave without me. But no, they'd help. I gave
my son the phone, practiced my father's instructions.

But nothing would work. I couldn't even connect
the phone call to my father. A voice came over
my own intercom. Voice interrupting. Asking me

what would happen if I missed this plane. What
would happen? I would have to stay, or find another
flight. And what luck to be both father and son.

Who Will Save, Now You're Grown

Fall's bank-drop, jukebox colors piling up.
Once down, James Brown, shuffle and split. Wind wears
the mounds away, moonwalking through, slap
happy spinning, brief red then yellow flares.

Leaves, good as money. *Dollar, dollar bill*—
younger you'd trade me red for ghost pipe,
corpse plant, orange bought fallen nests—quick skill,
craft, calculation—yellow tapped apples, knife-

carved wedges, Christ-eye centers, pip and stars.
The slide into piles, tick check, grass stain, one time
per annum, fixed rate, rake. Long boulevards
of trunks and stumps seemed stop gaps, the sublime

uselessness carting the drop would prove. Whose will
broke bank those afternoons? Agreed, we stood still.

My Father's Rooms

It's a morning when my love doesn't text.
My children, nearly men, are still asleep.
Late. They sleep late. One in the shallow

winter sunlight, his double bed facing east.
The other, younger, lies under the low
ceiling downstairs. Behind him packed

earth, skeletal rhododendron, graded
landscape; in front, sliding glass doors gape
before a frozen pond. Sunday morning.

I'm in the cold carport, someone else's
house, sublet, careful with my trash, cup
of coffee. I douse uncertainty in snow.

Thinking of my father, in his winter
off-season motels, voyaging from room
to room, beach town to beach town.

The same smell of bleach and sample
shampoo, pat of soap from a packet,
mold in every bathroom. Buzz and glow

of cable TV, his single luxury, the news
while dressing. Instant coffee, powdered
creamer, red stir-stick. He sips his cup

before work, while all of his children
sleep ranged across the rooms still
cleaned by their mother. He works

every day. He waits to call his girlfriend
from a payphone on the boardwalk,
the folding door salt-scuffed, key-carved,

hearts, kids' initials, four-letter words.
A surfer passes zipping his wetsuit, tugs
a balaclava, neoprene lid. My phone might

sigh and vibrate across the nightstand
inside. What world have I entered? I'm here,
single, my children sleeping. Almost men.

Connecticut River Report

I'm jumping ship. We've keeled the shallows, beached
along pacific rims that idle east
of urgency, and old idioms won't work here.
The tide is always changing near the Berkshires.

We've measured quite a bit more mass than weight—
and run aground where steeples prick the nape
of dusk beyond the bridge. The law's mosaic,
an orthodoxy of bits and pieces, cracked

contingencies a sort of sexy gear.
The tightest seal's on the subliminal here:
an astronaut turned poet laureate snaps
his boots across the sky, his leather chaps

and halter burning. His end is comedy,
one side effect of zero gravity.

Most Embarrassing Stories

We were telling our most embarrassing stories. Mine? I was running in the woods about a mile from my house when I swallowed a fly. Glad I can't see myself: big *duh*-mouth. Face like a feeding trout. Trotting and puffing, dumb-galooting up the hill toward a blackberry bush I'd been raiding for days. The bear spirits must have been pissed off: I'd picked it clean. Ha ha, trot trot, *pfff pfff.* Next thing I know, I'm coughing on a fly.

Only, it wasn't a fly. It was a yellow jacket. By the time I hawked it up into my hand—and it flew off, untroubled—it had stung the hell out of my throat. Luckily I wasn't allergic to bees. At least, hadn't been. My throat started to tighten—but that could have been a topical reaction, not necessarily systemic. Just in case, I booked it home. Called the doctor, who called an ambulance.

High on adrenaline, I did horizontal stand-up for the EMTs, rocked the gurney. Dumb shit I'd done in my life: surfing in a hurricane, swimming the Rahway River downstream from Merck, running past a grazing moose, driving the Jersey Turnpike on Benadryl, chasing a purse-snatcher down a Paris alley where his friends were waiting, hitchhiking across the old East Germany to Berlin. Don't worry, an EMT said. You'll survive this too. Worst-case scenario, we go in through here. He tapped near my Adam's apple. We can do a tracheotomy right here in the ambulance. That shut me up. Propped on the gurney, I watched out the back window, cars pulling over, everything receded: house and family and neighbors, the oaks and sycamores on our street, redbrick facades of downtown Amherst, my favorite bookstore, friend Nat at the desk, the tall dorms, skyscraping library at the University where I work, the graveyard with Shahid Ali's tomb. They didn't have to cut me—just jacked me with a blast of epinephrine when I went into shock, heartbeat crashing below thirty.

But that last bit? I didn't get to tell that. Cate was horror-mirthing through her hands. Tracheotomy! Hollie recited from her *Survival Guide*. Could have been worse, she said. Someone used a pen to trache a choking victim in Berkeley. The patient nearly died at the table. Then they were off and running, stories of survival.

In conversation with myself I remained philosophical. Give me a spectacular death. Or at least a dignified one. No bathroom accident, choking on a cracker. Let my legacy be startling, a story my children tell their children, my friends tell their friends. Cougar attack. Plane crash. Car bomb, quick if not commanding, sudden as a blown tire, thorough as drowning. Trampled by a horse. Beheaded by a falling window. BLM protest, truncheons plunging, I'm cold-cocked from behind by riot cops. No whitening of gray cells through twilight, fog-horning my son, mistaking him for my brother, demanding, What's happening to me?

FOUR • DOMESTIC DIRECT

Domestic Retrograde

The hummingbird hovered in the kitchen, wrong
side of the door, thudded the glass, stopped

all talk. Our boys drew at the table. I chopped
garlic at the counter. You filled wineglasses

near the sink. The bird in place, everyone
still. More fish swimming the damp June air

than god of war striking a wall, stoking
its foundry of anger and desire—helmeted, snake-

waving Huitzilopochtli, one of your subjects,
devotions, however ironic, maybe half, maybe

less. Wings nearly invisible, a crucifix hologram,
posture held static, petitioning, priestlike, green

back, black and red throat, hardly
the reincarnated warrior, syncretic Mars—

the wars were elsewhere, Donbas, Libya,
Afghanistan, elsewhere, far from our kitchen.

And then everyone moved. I billowed a tea
towel, some Sifnian souvenir, Apollonian

sunburst, gently covered the bird mid-air,
asked you to open the door, in one motion he was

liberated, flying back to the feeder. I wanted you
to love me. I could calm, pacify Mars. I thought

I did it for you. Before the war came
to us, before I knew we were fighting it.

Spontaneous Midnight Makeover Party

Can you believe outside the frame our kids
are sleeping through that revel? Boys keep swinging
while Alex mixes glammed-up dust for eyelids,
cheekbones, and lips. Here's Bill—young Bowie— synching,

Alex's one success. (What would you expect?
His training came on porno-sets, the trick
of covering acne on the ass, the oiled chest.)
The beauty's all Bill's, though: however thick

the orange rouge and coral gloss, the green
tornado-sky shadow over everyone's eyes—
here even I'm shined up, that's me, Miss Spleen—
Bill's unconcealed. The dress just amplifies

the man it fits—elegant neck, washboard and pecs,
all *clair-obscur*, this photo and the next.

Late to Saint Pat's / Domestic Direct

Mahal, my beloved, in a minute I'll play
Hennessy to your O'Shea, take down
my mother's Medusa, unclasp St. Anthony
medallion—and keep away from mirrors.

There's Guinness in the fridge, draft cans
with hollow clacking canisters, a fire
in the grate, and I can muster up
some Dubliners or Chieftains reel,

a surge of blarney from the SoundBar.
I'll tell you yes again about meeting
Spider Stacy, tin whistle-player
for the Pogues, my first trip to London.

How he whumped off his barstool, sack
of ripe corn cobs, when the rest of us
blinked—we were so tucked in—I stopped
all conversation to hoist him in a cab.

Turned back to beer and talk, the brick
of Ralph Ellison's *Invisible Man.*
Didn't find out who he was until we'd
long drunk him under and out of the bar.

                    •

Tamer days now. And abuse for phobic Cardinal
Dolan—I boycott his parade. Bring me
that Dubliners double LP, sing whiskey
in the jar. Downtown they're drinking

green lager. Here we're boiling the dinner
with rice. Our kids are cracking homework
in headphones, Earl Sweatshirt, Frank Ocean.
They've colonized the kitchen table. This age,

we won't be spreading the Diaspora
any further, but it'll be our pleasure later
to go through the motions. Settle here
next to me. This rotten couch that weathered

all your adolescent spring-times in Manila,
its crushed velvet—like us—as brown
as green, wet dog smell, stout spill, soot from
the poker, see where I've made room for you.

Sifnos Travelogue

From the ferry, the island looks denuded.

Smooth volcanic peaks all sun firing
across a yellow skull. Disembark. You begin
to see that flora here is cunning, vines

shift along every available crack
in stone, tamarisks line the beach, olive trees
strike low and orderly up on terraces, roots

dug deep. The people living here
are pretty clever too, houses propose
clean lines, square angles, a series of unfolding

cubes, thick-walled to be cool in summer,
warm in winter, and painted uniformly
white, shutters a strict palette, blue,

green, brown, one quick pink, blue and white
domes of churches—a chapel for every day
of the year, sanctum for every six Sifnians—

speckle each inhabited hillside, shrubs, pines,
and fruit trees surround the buildings, taut figs,
lemons, oranges, pomegranates, and limes,

cascading bougainvillea, banks of flowering capers,
shady grape arbors, night blooming jasmine,
enormous geraniums, feathery mimosas

rise beside pink-blossomed almond trees.
Farmers trawl fields, tend patches, cut
wild spices, karpouzi, peponi, melitzana

vlita, rigani, sofos, chorta, okra. Ladders
disappear into peach branches, orchards
give way to pasture, to chickens pecking, roving

goats, sheep grazing, the odd pig or cow
poking. Occasional animals in saddle or harness
harrow their tasks or stall in attitudes

of sublime passive aggression. How is it
that even here, in this season of paradise, austere
in its beauty, persistent despite *austerity*,

it's possible to shift, become one such
jackass, shuttered, sudden, hoof-
bent on refusal, eyes turned from the sea,

visible from every inch of the island,
blue,
      blue,
            blue,
                  blue? Now, neither
donkey nor rider, I've gone grey in the blue.

Across my love's wineglass rim, her friend's husband
aims his phone, moment digitally fixed. They laugh,
lean in, and I miss it, too busy welcoming you.

Idios

Past the tamarisk grove and night-blooming moon flowers,
private parking. Blue-green sparkling of the deep-water port.
Table for one, fried calamari and red sauce, a plate of vlita,

steamed weeds. Too early to breathe the jasmine, drink
white wine, amplify bouzouki. Too early to spring yourself
from yourself by drastic measure. All those weeks silent,

meditation and bridge-walking, white noise of river-crossing.
Back to self. Too much waiting, but what else to do but
wait? Welcome the end of the Aegean, a weighted blanket,

welcome the fishermen and sponge-divers, net bag
and bucket, baskets of spiky urchin, Lydia and Thea
lowering their sails, washing the decks, faint smell

of bleach and carmine, voices the briefest instructional
hum, telling you what, do what? Turn out, outside
where sunlight's antiseptic, saltwater sanitizing,

where the sky and sea meet in an indifferent or just imprecise
horizon. *Pateroúlis*, someone calls over your shoulder. Daddy.
Waking you to what? Grief? Love? Anxiety? A game of diving,

diving and retrieving, red plastic shovel the waves
threaten to bury. And once again you're pulling it
from the water in no great hurry, handing it back,

as if saving it from the sand and sea were necessary.

Lisbon / Transient Global Amnesia

Lisbon, you've hurt me, tricked
me into believing all the old lies.

Delusions are endless.

If you're looking for a mark, here
I am, flat on my hospital bed, joking against

amnesia, transient, global, while
my son stands by in terror. I told him

it felt like an acid flashback, there was
a buzzing in my brain, apologized

for his chromosomes, forgot
and apologized again. His mother's shadow

circled like a summoner, birdwing
petulance, all the elegance of crow's

flight, called back after she'd flown
to an intrigue's heights. I filed my own

missing person's report. Still I grouse, land
me, because this is about you, Lisbon,

because you waited for us. This return.
My son's along and laughing, memory

back and every labyrinth
open, your pink walls and pink

streets I wake and dream down.
At the end of every looted marble

sidewalk, under the sky of Igreja
de Sao Domingos, the clean halls

and coffee roast, machine oil
of Rossio Station, Alameda's uphill

tracks, along the plane trees
and at the top of every miradouro

I see you, your hands take hold
of me. I kiss your palms in this

second, this new Lisbon we
plant and pave for each other.

Lucid Even in Your Fury

What elegant shapes your mother staked
you to, lemniscate waist, ouroboran key,
such long thin wrists, delicate ankles, twee
Praxitelean feet. A mind no snake
could ever swallow. Your father made her suffer
the pique of familiar hurt and jealousy,
his charm the shifting fulcrum between you three.
You swore you'd write, eclipse his brightest lover.

And now you have. You're lucid even in
your fury, strangely gentle, patient with me,
while I'm as clabber sour, *naminam* sweet,
as any of your characters. I nod Protean,
fish-hook, blue eye, beloved palimpsest—
dark radiance, multivalent—someone's left.

Bitterness

Who or what climate change will melt
the icecaps of my bitterness? What hole
is deep enough to swallow this hole, swallow
my bitter swallowing of bitterness? What

syntax contain or convey my bitterness,
what form of address formal
and flexible enough to address the I
and Thou of bitterness, which person, which plural

intimate enough to know and discourse with
the necessary simplicity this complex root-
network linking the trees of my bitterness?
Why am I organ-harvesting it, opening

it vulture-wide with each sunset flight? Who
in bitterness approaches me, who comes
awaited, incanted to or against, summoned,
conjured, prayed for, what explosives planted

to break the concrete walls damming, hydraulics
spinning, electrifying the hills and valleys
carved by that river of bitterness, confluence of rivers,
what harbor, gulf, sea, ocean settling finally the silt

of bitterness? The Greenland shark, its half-
millennium of bitterness, slow swimming,
thick-gilled, dead-eyed, rough-skinned?
Or sea-lions in tide-pools, sunning on

the rocks of bitterness? Who sits inside
the mouth of what whale bitterly
praying to their bitter God, or is it
another holy story ruined by bitterness,

cartooned into another son's bitter
sacrifice, burning a wooden puppet
who would be a real boy, and the burning is
the only return from bitterness, is that the point?

What bitter passing, what desert is dry
enough to vaporize such bitterness so fully
no cloud could ever consume and store it,
could ever rain it back down over us, love?

I'd Be the Fish

What would satisfy, he asks, and I can hardly say.
Her story, I'm the fish swimming through it
from line to line. But the terrain's too dry, no way
to brook this drought. City-planner, then, she drew it

near floodplains, I'm irrigation from the Nile,
canals that fill Venice's green lagoon.
Let her be bank and island, from marble tile
to god's-eye atrium. I'll flow and drone,

a constant murmur. Nah, you're a racket, horn
and whistle, thorn and thistle. Fish? A shark
at best, three sets of teeth, and nothing born
above or below survives your ocean's dark—

better admit it now. Expect nothing, accept
less. Swim uncertainty, dorsal fixed, tail flexed.

He sounds so sure. Socratic? Delphic. Stark.

After Greece

Your leaving felt like returning
from a month in Greece, sea salt

still stiffening my hair, drying my skin
against mosquitoes, happy, if skin

can be happy, and dark
as my grandfather's, no more

tamarisk shade and katabatic
wind, cool meltemi, all left behind

for others with the chilled
carafe half full of local white wine,

spiral of condensation rings,
and how many glasses, how many

waiting, enduring in hunger the smell
of goat mastelo slow cooking in clay pots,

lamb chops grilling, small hard lemons
cut and quartered in a blue bowl, ready,

weedy green chorta low boiling, potatoes
frying in olive oil, all, like you

closer in the past to me than the future,
who knows when we'll be back again,

lope home with our arms around each other
after dinner, brush against the rosemary bush

on the way back to the terrace, up
the *steno*, mimosa tree black and pink

under the grey-green light of an old lamppost,
thyme I've clipped with a knife along the cliff path

drying on the counter, I'll turn back
the sheets while you shutter

the windows, quieting the Vespa sputter
fading up the hill to Apollonia—

the sound was in my own mouth, a noise I
was making, failing to distract

myself, entirely unaware of anything
but you everywhere here.

Some Future Tense

What if every kiss she gives me replaces
one you didn't? Every time she touches
my arm, my neck, the blades

of my hips, small of my back,
diminishes some time
we didn't touch? Whenever she

leans close wearing the sandalwood
she knows I like, tells me she loves
me, fills our silence around love?

Or helps forget a conversation about fishing
for bream and mullet on Sark. Or bringing biscuits
to visit huts in Botswana. Or watching pink

river dolphins from your berth in Peru. Or
the tribal wars and martial cunning
that got Magellan stabbed, the beach on Mactan

off Cebu, or the criminal Alexander Pearce
captured in Van Diemen's Land with his pockets
full of human flesh, or young Jim Jones selling

monkeys door to door, or the character
in one of your books who killed and ate
her boyfriends or another who was knighted

then hanged for treason or another
who pushed her husband off a cliff
in Hydra, the cliff above the spot where you

first told me about this book seven years
before you wrote it. Or it's sailing through
sharks in the Swann River in your childhood

or crashing the coup at the Manila Hotel
in high school for packets of free peanuts
and beer. Another time our lips didn't

move. I'm looking forward to when—
when?—our old silence is nothing
like the water around my head

as I snorkel over a red octopus
contorted under rocks, weever
bolting in the sand, loggerhead turtle

passenger beside me, and the kiss she
gives me in the Algarve shade
is just one more she gave me.

Which God?

I Which God Were You?

Which God were you? The one
who bathed me in the kitchen sink
when I was small enough to fit?

Who made the camel kneel
and the cow low? Who drove the fish
up the canal to spawn under

piers that reeked of creosote?
Who blessed and cursed me
with the dream of fidelity?

Who wore the ice caps like
a fool's hat, who drove the clown car?
Who made a Calvary of sumac

blasting from the pavement?
Who blazed out with the Chanukkah candles
before bed then cut the Christmas lights?

Who stroked me under the covers
when the fever hit and sleep slept?
Who reminds me I'm both father and son

and splits the sky unevenly between
the day and night? Who covers darkness
with a deeper dark? Who wakes me

with the light? Bathe me with the light.

II Closer to God

I tried through love of my wife
to get closer to God, love for family,
our children, each bath and spoonful

of sweet potato, each shoulder stack
or piggy-back, each kiss, my left arm
bulging with muscle as I carried one

or the other, my right doing the work
of feeding and teaching, cleaning
and soothing. When the crying came

I held them through it, when
the walking, helped them walk
knowing they would walk away.

•

What cis male even says that anymore, *wife*—
and God? And where are you, skin bathed
in jasmine smoke or myrrh, eyes open, kneeling

each morning, the trash bin cleared
of vegetable rot, lemons squeezed
to rind and seed, dry chicken bones. These

offerings to the sun and hunger
and thirst and silence stave off
what, bring you closer to what?

•

I don't know. The sawmill across the street
grinds out the morning, the cows pasturing
beside it wander and gather near the woods'

edge. Hushed cars pass, and logging trucks.
It's far from where I started, the paint
factory and chem-plant, the refineries

along Route One. I come closer, closer
to the blank gods of these hills, filtered
sunlight, brown farmland. The tree crowded

with starlings sharpens, as a hawk
passes over. For now my head's a stadium
full of silence, a quiet congregation.

III Twenty Questions

Who is the you behind the you
you revive every morning and follow out
into sun covered in fog, under white pines

and over bridges crossing cold
flowing streams, rivers of snow melt?
When you board the train willingly

with a letter that begins, I don't wish
I'd never met you, do those double
negatives negate your shame

and suffering? When you plunge up
the tracks, pass the mountains of your lost
New England shangri-la, your past

and family and dissolution of what mattered
most to you, do you keep your eyes averted
or do you watch the stopped mills

and sullen bricks? When you see
a raccoon on the flat factory roof do you
turn to your seatmate and include them

in the marvel? Or do you stop up
your ears with buds, and how will
those buds flower? Into song,

speech, music without words?
What do you ask yourself as coffee
brews in the back and you smell

pastries in the microwave, the café
car and its offerings, and you remember
Malcolm X worked the cross country trains?

As did your father's uncles, and their
father and uncles, and theirs, and on back?
How do you board and sit and watch

and listen, leaving behind the ruined cities
you track through? How do you keep
quiet? How do you see the stilled

cranes, the rusted machinery of childhood
that has yet to be cleared, the human
lives in buses and cars and on foot

passing by still, or waiting at the bus stops,
waiting at the stations of these former
sites of industry and bust, these Camdens

and Amboys, Bridgeports and Holyokes?
Who are you and how do you pass through
and how is it the best you can hope for is

that someone writes I don't wish I'd never
met you, what have you ever done? What will
you do now? Where and how will you get off,

beside which mill or factory, which storage tank
or coker unit, where will you find the refinery
intended for the soul? The one that burns through

the self? That will finally change this world?

After Alexandria

What an agony not to wake up next to you.
Not to have fallen asleep with your head on my chest.

I made the bed quickly, as you did every day,
sheets that smell, still, of your hair and skin,
pillows, one that you took with you, take
with you everywhere, sandalwood to the feathers.

Coffee solo but not alone, son painting inside, landlord
fixing, planing the screen door. And this note to you,
who are here in my head like a razor folded in its case.

Acknowledgments

Asian Signature: "Pay Packet Saturday," "Leading with My Wedding Ring," and "Lucid Even in Your Fury"

ASP Bulletin: "Living the Dream" and "I'd Be the Fish"

Bear Review: "Panic Through the Refineries"

Bennington Review: "Twenty Questions"

The Best American Poetry 2024: "Domestic Retrograde"

Ethos Literary Journal: "After Alexandria" and "Most Embarrassing Stories"

Fulcrum: an annual of poetry and aesthetics: "Cerberus vs. Freddy"

Green Mountains Review: "Middle School and Son" and "Crane Elegy"

Hampden-Sydney Poetry Review: "Bitterness"

Hanging Loose: "Idios"

Harvard Review: "After Greece"

Italian Americana: "Open Season, 2016"

Massachusetts Review: "Family Man in the Valley," "Oil Tank Farm," "Tutor to the Prophet," and "In Another Life"

Matter: "Domestic Retrograde" and "Lisbon / Transient Global Amnesia"

Poetry: "Convenience Store Aquinas," "Netflix Green Man," and "More Sky Please"

Poetry Ireland Review: "Family Story / So What Dad"

Poetry Northwest: "Who Will Save, Now You're Grown"

The Poetry Review: "Convenience Store Aquinas" (reprint)

Poetry at Sangam: "Whiskey Green Man" and "Silvano"

Salt: "Connecticut River Report"

Southern Poetry Review: "Leaving the Garden"

Southwest Review: "No Clock in the Forest"

St. Petersburg Review: "Miguel Hernandez Green" and "My Father's Rooms"

Tampa Review: "Some Future Tense"

The Wolf: "Back Home"

The Yale Review: "Spontaneous Midnight Makeover Party"

Thanks

This book began as something completely different, one reason it took time to finish, and now there are many people to THANK:

Ru Freeman, who offered helpful suggestions on every level, from the line to the collection as a whole. Thank you for all your tender care and tough cuts.

Lawrence Joseph, for reading several drafts, making keen line-edits, and offering enormous help with the structure. Your conversation has been sustaining.

Mary Jo Salter, long-time friend and a source of generosity not just to me but to many, for your gimlet eye on the level of the line to the overall structure of this collection.

Nathan McClain and JJ Starr, for help with the individual poems as well as the book, and for our many late-night conversations during its composition.

Christine Lysnewycz Holbert, for shepherding this book into the world.

Sunetra Gupta, for being an early reader of many of these poems and a constant source of friendship and support.

Burlin Barr, for reading early drafts of many poems here, always ready for the long-haul conversation, always entered into fearlessly.

"Jagu" Jagannathan, Brad Leithauser, and Sheila McCormick, core members of the A(O)DC, even during the pandemic.

Maria de Caldas Antão and Pierre Hoonhout, for their conversation and extraordinary hospitality, their ability to create an international community and nurturing environment wherever they are.

Nicholas and Gabriel Carlos, for their inspiration and a variety of aspirations. Of course, John Sr., Terry, Mary, Patty, Kathy, Lisa, Danny, Bryan, TJ, RJ. Global family, especially Ian, Helena, Liz, Charlie.

The many artists whose conversations have helped in the composition of this book, including Polina Barskova, Vievee Francis, Stephen Haven, Skip and Patty Hays, Matthew Hicks, Major Jackson, Ostap Kin, Virginia Konchan, Scott Laughlin, Kevin O'Connor, Jeff Parker, Kevin Stewart, Zack Strait, my brother Hyon Gak Sunim and the sangha, Natasha Trethewey.

Soundtrack of thanks:

ABBA, All Them Witches, Natacha Atlas, Bee Gees, Blue Hawaii, Bombino, David Bowie, The Breeders, Bryan Jonestown Massacre, Maria Callas, Cairokee, Jim Carroll, Channel Tres, Chromatics, George Clanton, Cold Cave, Bootsy Collins, Daft Punk, Pino D'Angio, Claude Debussy, Depeche Mode, Amr Diab, Stratos Dionysiou, Thomas Dolby, Pete Dougherty, The Doves, Drake, Ekkah, Eli Escobar, Fairuz, The Fall, Fennesz, Neil Frances, Fun Boy Three, Funkadelic, Alison Goldfrapp, Peggy Gou, Holy Ghost!, Andrew Huang, Jessica Six/Nomi Ruiz, Grace Jones, Jungle, The Juan Maclean, Junior Boys, Kaytranada, Kraftwerk, Kendrick Lamar, Kaskade/Late Night Alumni, King Tubby, Little Dragon, SG Lewis, Luxxury, M.I.A., Madredeus, Major Lazer, Marinella, Mario, Mazzy Star, Miami Horror, George Michael, Mina, Giorgio Moroder, Munya, Roisin Murphy, Klaus Nomi, Johnny Osbourne, Opal, Otha, Park Hye Jin, Parliament, Man Parrish, Part Time, Peaches, Lee "Scratch" Perry, Pet Shop Boys, The Pixies, The Pogues, Poolside, Tony Pops, Prince, Lana Del Rey, Nile Rodgers, Robyn, Roosevelt, Röyksopp, Ryuchi Sakamoto, Erik Satie, Travis Scott, Sally Shapiro (Johan Agebjörn), Shit Robot, Sam Sparro, Stereolab, The Stooges, Sylvester, Timecop1983, Toro y Moi, U.S. Girls, Ultraflex, Luther Vandross, Anna Vissi, Jessie Ware, The Warlocks (Bobby Hecksher), John Wayne, The Weeknd, Nancy Whang, Wire, Wolfsheim, Hande Yener...

—Epigraph from Serhiy Zhadan, translated by John Hennessy and Ostap Kin

JOHN HENNESSY is the author of two previous collections, *Coney Island Pilgrims* (Ashland Poetry Press) and *Bridge and Tunnel* (Turning Point Books), and his poems appear in *The Best American Poetry 2024, The Believer, The New Republic, Poetry, Poetry Ireland Review,* and *The Yale Review.* With Ostap Kin he is the translator of *A New Orthography* (also from Lost Horse Press), selected poems by Serhiy Zhadan, finalist for the PEN Award for Poetry in Translation and co-winner of the Derek Walcott Prize, the anthology *Babyn Yar: Ukrainian Poets Respond* (Harvard Library of Ukrainian Literature), and *Set Change,* selected poems by Yuri Andrukhovych (NYRB/ Poets Series). Hennessy is the poetry editor of *The Common* and teaches at the University of Massachusetts, Amherst.